Contemporary Candlemaking

WILLIAM E. WEBSTER WITH CLAIRE McMULLEN

DOUBLEDAY & COMPANY, INC.
GARDEN CITY, NEW YORK
1972

EDITORIAL DIRECTOR, RACHEL MARTENS
PHOTOGRAPHY, AL J. REAGAN
CANDLES BY WILLIAM E. WEBSTER (EXCEPT AS CREDITED)

ISBN-0385-00775-2
LIBRARY OF CONGRESS CATALOG CARD NUMBER 72-84974

CONTENTS

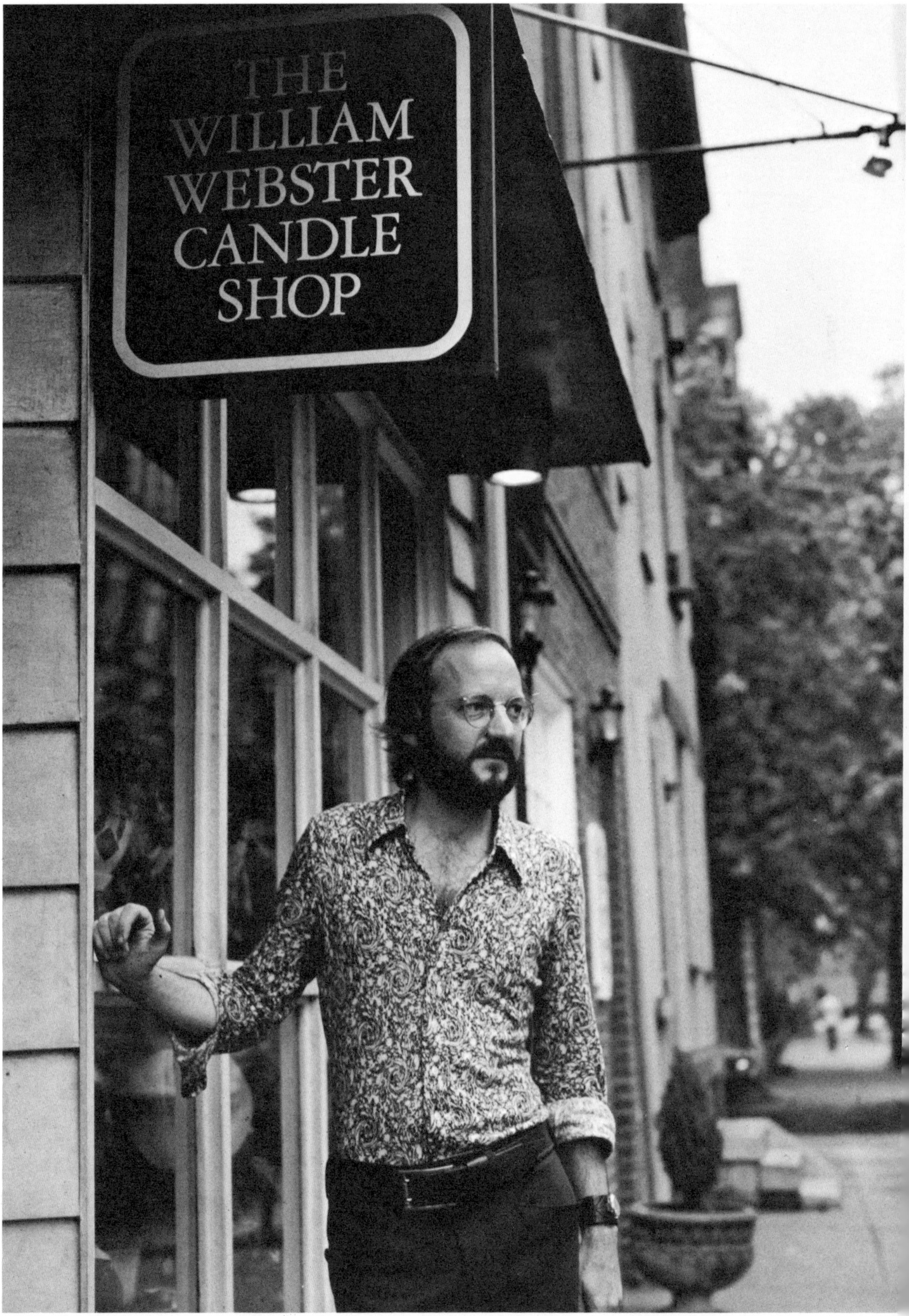
THE
WILLIAM
WEBSTER
CANDLE
SHOP

INTRODUCTION

Candlemaking is a craft and, potentially, an art. The intent of this book is to provide you with the technical skills of the craft.

In addition, we have tried to convey the excitement of working with wax and letting your own imagination expand its creative possibilities.

A candle itself scarcely needs defining except to observe that it must be made of wax and a wick. The primary property of a burning candle is flickering light. Time and legend have endowed candlelight with an aura of symbolism and romance that is, perhaps, the secret of the eternal appeal of candles and the popularity of candlemaking.

There are different types of candles—those made commercially by machine, dipped candles and poured candles. In this book we are concerned only with poured candles because it is these which provide greatest variety and respond best to the demands of imagination.

The pouring method of candlemaking is applicable to a variety of candle types and the most important of these are covered in individual chapters. For each type there will be certain differences in the materials and techniques required. How well you handle these techniques determines the quality of your finished candle. Standards of excellence are included to help you judge the results of your own work. Appear at end of chapters featuring candle techniques.

I believe there is obvious similarity between candlemaking and architecture. Both are structural, both are judged visually on the selection and use of combined materials. But just as a building must accommodate people, so, too, a candle must burn. Usefulness is the final judgment of quality. This conviction explains the subject matter I have elected to cover in this book.

You may wonder at the omission of candle holders, arrangements and most applied external decorations. The reason is clear and, I hope, provocative. These things are not part of the candle, just as landscaping is not a structural part of architecture. We are concerned primarily here with candle structure. As a craftsman, your objective is to create a candle to function as an entity in wax. Adornments such as real or artificial flowers or fruit, sequins and other glitter, are unrelated to the basic nature and purpose of the candle. Our approach to decoration is entirely structural and generic—that is, we look to the versatility of wax for aesthetic values as well as function.

Step-by-step instructions in each chapter include professional techniques that will help the amateur to pour candles comparable to the finest available in many shops today. So candlemaking can be a profitable hobby as well as a creatively satisfying one.

We have tried to make this book a basic course in candlemaking, detailing the skills which, when mastered, will make you an accomplished craftsman. Your own imagination, plus the skill to execute your ideas, will earn you the status of an artist with wax.

William E. Webster

MATERIALS AND CRAFTSMANSHIP
CHAPTER 1

Your medium is wax and its versatility will continue to unfold for as long as you make candles. To know the capabilities of your medium is the essence of craftsmanship. You learn by experimenting and, in the end, your own original theories produce finished works that are distinctively your own creations.

In the beginning, all you really have to know is that most hobby shops sell candle wax in 10- or 11-pound slabs. While this might seem to be a large quantity, it will be gone very quickly once you begin to pour. If there is no hobby shop in your area you may shop by mail, using the directory of suppliers at the end of this book.

One important thing to remember is that the paraffin sold in grocery stores may have a variety of household uses, but it does not make usable candles. Always ask for and use candle wax, which is fully refined paraffin, formulated to burn safely, without smoking.

Candle wax comes in varieties which melt at different temperatures. There are three basic classes of melt point waxes: 125° to 130°, 140° to 145° and 150° to 160°. These will be referred to as low, medium and high melt point wax, respectively. (All temperatures throughout the book are Fahrenheit.) The significance is that higher melt point wax is harder wax and makes slower burning candles. This is important for wax which is to be non-burning. Some of the candles discussed in this book have wax which is not to be consumed by the flame; such wax is referred to as non-burning wax. If you can find only low melt point wax you'll still be able to make these candles since there are additives to raise the melt point. We cover these shortly.

If the melt point is not indicated on the wax you buy, you can test it yourself. Put a small chunk into a pan and insert a candy or deep fat thermometer into the wax when it melts. Remove the pan from the burner and let the wax cool. Check the temperature at the time the wax begins to crystallize and solidify. That's the melt point. You need not run this test unless you're making a candle requiring hard, non-burning wax such as the shell of a hurricane candle (Chapter 8).

The temperatures mentioned in each chapter are pouring temperatures, that is, the heat of your melted wax at the time you actually pour a candle. The suggested pouring range is between 170° and 250°. Standard pouring temperature will be 195°; this is attainable in a double boiler. A lower temperature pouring is indicated for a mold which cannot withstand temperatures above 160°. Pouring temperatures above 210° (usually not exceeding 240°) are primarily for sand candles when a thick wall of sand is desired.

How much wax should you buy? Well, a candle 6 inches high and 3 inches in diameter weighs about 1½ pounds. You can work up and down the scale from that point. Or you can measure how much water your mold holds and melt sufficient wax to equal that amount in liquefied state. (Be sure to dry the mold thoroughly before pouring wax.)

WAX ADDITIVES

I recommend that when you begin to make candles, you do so without adding anything to the wax you buy. But, as your skill increases, so will your standards and ambition. Eventually, you'll want to consider these additives:

HARDENING-WHITENING CRYSTALS: small plastic pellets which will raise the melt point and increase the opacity of your wax. Epolene, made by Eastman-Kodak, is one type. Available in small quantities in some hobby shops, Epolene is inexpensive to use because you add only 1 teaspoon for every 2 pounds of wax. We consider hardening crystals, such as Epolene, superior to stearic acid as a strengthener because ½ teaspoon of crystals will raise the melt point of a pound of wax about 5 degrees. It would take many times this amount of stearic acid to achieve the same effect. Epolene produces a glossy, marble-like finish (whether white or with color); stearic acid produces a cloudy, chalky finish. Crystals must melt to be effective. Add them sparingly; too many will make the candle burn poorly and reduce its glow.

If Epolene is not available in your area, other hardening-whitening crystals are adequate and most are superior to stearic acid. Incidentally, stearic acid is not to be confused with "pure stearin" candles from Denmark. These are some of the finest candles produced in the world.

HARDENING-WHITENING CRYSTALS

WAX-BASE DYES: available in solid state, liquid and powder form. I recommend solid for your first venture into color. (Follow instruction on package.) You can experiment with liquid and powdered color later, when you've mastered the fundamentals of candle pouring. In time, you'll be able to mix your own dyes.

Should you want to mix two colors, always add the lighter one first. To test the solidified color of your molten wax, place 1½ inches in a white cup and let it cool. If you decide to add more color, test it again before pouring.

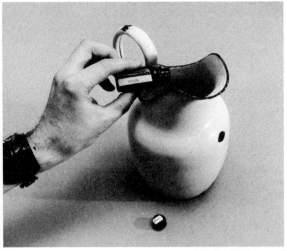

OIL-BASE SCENTS

OIL-BASE SCENT: adds another dimension to your finished candle. Almost any aroma you can think of is available in concentrated liquid form or in scent pellets—florals, spices, even coconut. Add scent to wax in the pitcher just before pouring; or you may add scent to the repour only; or you can dip the wick in liquid scent before inserting it in the candle. But if you add liquid to the wax—and you can use your favorite perfume if it's oil-based—remember that a few drops, no more than ½ teaspoon, is enough to scent a 2- or 3-pound candle. Do not use plastic containers or utensils with scent. Burning aroma should be subtle, not overwhelming because scent is offensive to many people. In fact, if your candle is to be used at mealtimes, it's better to forget about adding scent.

BEESWAX will enhance the luster, natural aroma and texture of your candle and should be considered a wax blend, rather than an additive. If you use beeswax, keep it to 10 or 15 percent of your total wax mixture. Beeswax comes in 1-pound slabs and costs about ten times more than paraffin wax. For non-burning hurricane shells, I recommend a beeswax mixture plus hardening crystals.

WICKING

The wick affects the quality of your finished candle almost as much as the wax. You'll want a cotton wick when you're using a mold with a hole in the bottom so tension can be applied. Use a metal core wick when there can be no tension, when the wax has a low melt point or when it's to be inserted after the candle has hardened—as in sand and container candles. (See Chapter 3 for instruction.) Again your friendly hobby shop, or direct mail supplier, has wicking for sale by the spool or yard. Cotton string or twine is not a satisfactory substitute for regular candle wicking.

Wicking comes in different sizes; you can buy a standard small and large in both plain cotton and wire core. If the wick is too large, the candle will burn too quickly, smoke and run. Too-small, the wick will give too small a flame and cause the flame to drown itself in melted wax.

In sand candles—and when you're using improvised molds—you'll insert a *wick wire,* when the candle is forming. You'll replace this later with a *wire core wick.* Straightened metal coat hangers are ideal for this purpose. Cut lengths of assorted sizes, say from about 9 inches and up. The wire, when inserted, should stand above the level of the candles by about 6 inches so that you have enough of a handle to hold or maneuver it.

MULTIPLE WICKING

For candles with a top surface area of more than 3 inches across—round, square or oblong—you may prefer more than one wick for more efficient use of the wax. These will be candles you make in sand or improvised molds, rather than professional molds.

A wire core wick burns a larger diameter in softer wax (lower melt point wax) than it does in wax which has been hardened with crystals. The following guide is intended as a rule of thumb and is included prematurely here but you'll want to refer to it as you progress.

Melt Point of Wax	Wire Core Wick	Burning Diameter
145°	1 small	1¼ "
	2 small	3 "
135°	1 small	1½ "
	1 large	2 "

The burning diameter of multiple wicks is always greater than the sum of the separate wicks. If two small wicks are used they should be placed in the center of the candle, about 1 inch apart.

Ideal wicking for a permanent candle is to space wicks so that all wax will be consumed except for a ½-inch wall around the edge of the container. You can then renew the candle by repouring fresh wax—or dropping in ready-made refills.

MOLDS

An empty milk carton, bottle, muffin tin, gelatin mold, drinking glass—you name it—becomes a candle mold the minute you think it should.

On the other hand, your candlemaking repertoire should include graceful pillars and obelisks, sturdy cylinders, magnificent twice-poured stars. Metal molds are available for these shapes and others at candle supply shops.

Someday, you'll branch out to other shapes and create your own molds. Skeptical? See Chapter 6. But, basically, we're thinking throughout about only two kinds of molds—the commercial ones you can buy and the kinds you'll improvise.

First of all, choose your work space. Your workshop can be the kitchen or any free space in the house. A simple hot plate performs as well as the four-burner range.

Spread your work area with newspapers or any other throwaway cover. This will shorten clean-up time after every work session.

Now, break up your wax—I like a hammer for this—and put it into the double boiler and onto the stove to melt. You can improvise a double boiler by using a coffee can in a pan of water.

Melting wax takes about 90 percent of your candle-making time so, as a matter of routine, put the wax on to melt before doing anything else. Be sure to insert the thermometer in the pan as soon as the wax liquefies to prevent overheating. This is especially important when working over direct heat. While the double boiler is the suggested heating vessel for beginners, it does impose limitations in that the highest temperature your wax will reach is roughly 195°.

For pouring at higher temperatures, place wax directly over heat in a large saucepan or, better yet, a bucket. Never put a plastic or glass pitcher on direct heat.

BREAKING UP WAX

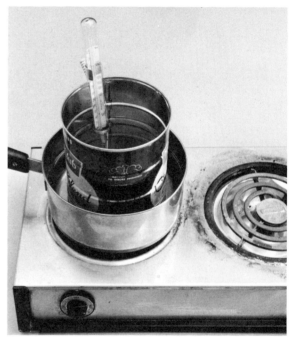

MELTING WAX (Double Boiler)

MELTING WAX (Direct)

POURING WAX

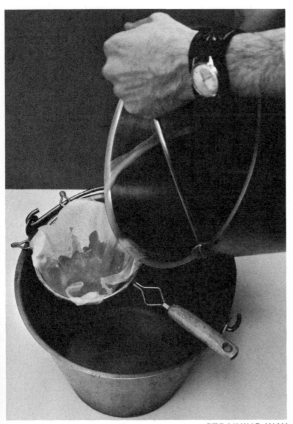

STRAINING WAX

When you melt wax directly over flame or an electric burner, always transfer it to a pitcher with an open spout before pouring into a mold. You'll have more control over the hot liquid. Use buckets and pitchers made of stainless steel or porcelain. Some metals, such as aluminum, may react adversely with the wax.

As you go about your other preparations, keep a watchful eye on the melting wax. If it drips or spills onto the stove, wipe up immediately with paper towels. Any container with a seam, especially coffee cans, will eventually lose wax. When coffee cans begin to leak discard them. Never put a coffee can or any container with a seam on direct heat.

Place all the equipment you intend to use within easy reach––pitcher, mold, wick, ice pick, color, scent. If a water bath is called for, fill the pan or bucket with water. Note that most of your candlemaking tools are ordinary household equipment. You can substitute anything that occurs to you, if it serves the purpose.

Now you're ready. You've learned the first step and it's the standard start for your every candlemaking adventure. I'll refer to these preparations as Standard Step One through the following chapters.

WHILE THE WAX IS MELTING

Let's set the ground rules for workmanship. Safety first. Liquid wax is a flammable material but not dangerous when you exercise normal care. This means: Keep an eye on wax as it melts . . . always use a thermometer . . . never pour near an open flame . . . keep stove and burners clean of any wax which might drop from containers or utensils.

Wax fires are not common but should you accidentally ignite liquid wax, don't attempt to douse it with water. Use baking soda or quickly put a lid on the pan. If you should spill hot wax on your skin, apply cold water to remove the wax and wash the skin with a mild soap. None of this precautionary advice should frighten you— these are just things you should know to become a competent, confident craftsman.

Cleanliness comes next. Dust or leftover wax in a mold will ruin the next candle you try to make in that mold. So will foreign particles in wax. The perfectionist will always strain wax, even when it's brand new. This is especially important when you use metal molds or when you're using leftover (remelted) wax in any mold. An easy way is to use a large food strainer with a facial tissue inside. Dip each corner of the tissue in hot wax and it will adhere to the metal rim of the strainer.

That completes the groundwork. You are ready to make your first candle.

ICE CANDLES
CHAPTER 2

STEP 2

Making an ice candle appears to involve magic—it looks difficult, but it isn't. The results never fail to evoke amazement because it works every time. It's the ideal candle for a beginner who wants to experience quick success.

Structurally, an ice candle involves inside space, made up of holes left by the ice, and outside space which will be a wall of wax opened at random in a pattern created by the melting ice. A second candle forms the core of an ice candle and this is the part which will burn.

For this, your first effort, you'll use the techniques basic to all candlemaking but you'll have results in less than an hour. Your candle will emerge from the mold decorated because ice is an abstract artist. You may add such touches as color dipping, or glass pieces to emphasize the holes, as you choose.

Ice candles are fragile—they wouldn't give you a profitable mail order business but their decorative value is high. The effect of moving flame heightens the structural relationship of core and shell and is a lovely sight. Ice candles also show you at once the principle of the hurricane candle—interior light through a non-burning shell. More about this in Chapter 7.

A word about molds: Use a milk carton, if you like, or any other container with a closed bottom. It should be at least 4 inches high. We're showing a metal hurricane mold which has no wick opening in the bottom. To begin, use an inexpensive dinner taper as a core candle. After you've learned to pour your own, use a pillar, or round, candle which is preferable to a taper because a taper will burn too quickly.

To make an ice candle you'll need:
    Mold
    1½ pounds of medium melt point wax, approx.
    Core candle (such as a dinner taper)
    Ice
    Hammer
    Pan for ice
    Plastic bag
    Water bath
    Skillet

Optional:
    Bucket for dipping
    Color
    Propane torch

STANDARD STEP 1
The pouring temperature can be anywhere between 180° and 210°. You'll get good results by pouring at 195°.

STEP 2
Center the core candle in mold. (Because this is a metal mold we've sprayed it quickly with silicone release, available in aerosol containers at hobby shops. This operation is pictured in Chapter 4.)

NOTE: Decide now whether the top of the mold will be the top or bottom of your finished candle. (The shape of the mold is the deciding factor.)

If the top of the mold is the top of the candle, pour wax of about ½-inch deep in the bottom of the mold. When it scums, insert the core candle in upright position. Let cool and then add ice. (This is an optional step; if you want holes all the way to the bottom of the candle, omit this ½-inch pour.)

If the bottom of the mold is the top of the candle, insert the core candle upside down and let the ice hold it in place. Remember to repour fairly quickly over the ice at the top of the mold if you want your finished candle to have a solid wax base.

Decorative possibilities for ice candles are unlimited: If you use a dark core candle, color will flow through the ice holes as it burns. Open up closed areas with a torch. For the red and white candle, pour both colors at the same time, using both hands. For another effect place color glass chips among ice pieces before pouring. Or return the finished candle to the mold for a second pouring of black wax to fill the holes left after the ice melts and water dries.

STEP 3
Place ice (cubes or cake) in a plastic bag and smash with hammer. Pour the cracked ice into the pan and select pieces to put into the mold. Small pieces will give lacy effect; large pieces work a more open design. You want irregular or ragged edges so don't use whole ice cubes.

STEP 4
Fill the mold with ice, up to the height of the core candle. If you want a solid top, bring ice to within 1 inch of the top of the core candle.

STEP 5
If the ice has started to melt, be sure to drain the excess water before filling the mold with wax. Pour the wax in immediately.

STEP 3

STEP 4

STEP 5

STEP 6

STEP 6

Place the filled mold in a room-temperature water bath. For this, use any container deep enough to allow the water level to equal the level of the wax in the mold. Put remaining wax back on the burner to stay warm. As a rule, ice candles don't require a repour but if you see a depression toward the center of the candle, repour wax to slightly below the height of the original pour. (If you' pour higher, hot wax will seep down along the sides of the mold and the surface of the candle will be marred. You'll also have difficulty removing it from the mold.) Let the mold remain in the water bath for about ½ hour. Remove when mold and wax are no longer warm to the touch.

STEP 7

Remove candle from mold, remembering that water will come out, too. If candle does not slide out easily, work the mold in your hands until you feel the candle release. If the candle still does not separate from the mold, place it in the refrigerator for about ½ hour. It should then slide out easily. Let the candle dry thoroughly (about 24 hours) before going on to following steps.

STEP 8

The candle may be finished to your liking just as it comes from the mold, or you may want to give the surface a softer, velvety effect. An in-and-right-out dip in a bucket of boiling water will round off jagged edges and soften the finish. A just-as-fast dip in hot wax (250°) will give a rich, mellow finish to the entire surface. Grasp the wick of the core candle as you dip.

STEP 7

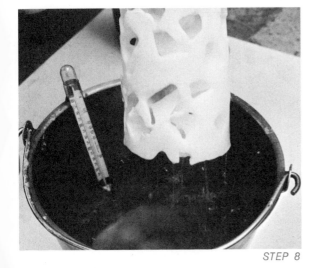

STEP 8

STEP 9

STEP 10

ADDED TOUCHES TO TRY

Color alone offers many decorative possibilities for ice candles. You can use a dark core with a white shell, or vice versa. Both core and shell may be the same color, in which case the candle takes on an intriguing look of being only one piece.

When you reach Step 8 you might elect to dip your shell into a colored wax (200°). The color surface effect will be enhanced by the interior light of the burning core candle.

For a completely different two-tone look, return your finished candle to the mold and pour colored wax (at a temperature of 170°) to fill in the holes. Place immediately in the water bath again until the mold and wax are cool to touch and then remove from mold.

Finally, experiment, experiment. Your imagination will set your candles apart from all others—and that's your goal.

STANDARDS OF EXCELLENCE

Your ice candle will look fragile but it should not crumble when touched. As it comes from the mold, the surface of the candle might show cracks from too-quick cooling, have rough edges that will break easily, or a harsh looking color and rough texture. All these flaws can be corrected by dipping the candle in a bucket of boiling water or hot (250°) wax. If the top of the candle is uneven, level it on a skillet as shown in Step 9.

The regularity of the holes left by the ice is important if your candle is to have a professional look. Holes that are only partially opened, as well as solid areas on the candle surface, should be opened with a propane torch.

In use, the burning core candle should glow through the outside candle, highlighting the surface finish and the pattern of holes. This interplay of inside-outside space is the drama of an ice candle.

STEP 9
To give your candle a level and stable base, place it on a skillet over low heat (225°). Rotate the candle gently and quickly with your palms. Do this with the top of the candle at your eye level. Remove from the skillet after a few seconds. If the candle is still not level, let it cool for a few minutes before you return it to the skillet and rotate again.

STEP 10 (optional)
Professional candlemakers consider a propane torch their most valuable tool. Here we're showing how to open up solid wax areas or holes where the ice did not fully penetrate the surface. (This happens at times to any craftsman.) Set the torch on low flame and apply the flame directly to the wax. Work lightly and patiently. Place the candle in a shallow container—or raise it over paper—to catch drippings.

Always wait about 24 hours to light a newly poured candle. This gives the wax a chance to settle down chemically and improves its burning quality. In this case the burning part of your candle was aged previously but it has come in contact with newly poured wax. So restrain yourself. Your light can shine tomorrow.

SAND CANDLES
CHAPTER 3

The creative structural possibilities of candles cast in sand are almost limitless and have hardly been explored. Sand candles were one of man's earliest light sources, but that function seems merely a primitive state compared with the expressive sand casting now being done —we show some designs in this chapter.

Once again you're creating space in candlemaking—the negative space of a hole dug in sand which you'll turn into a positive, functional, even permanent wax object. Properly constructed, sand candles can be used and repoured almost indefinitely.

Sand varies in color from the white of many beaches to the stunning black of the Snake River bed in northwest Wyoming. Try to find as many colors—and textures—as you can, even if you have to haunt the local masonry yards and construction sites. Very fine sand will give you a ceramic effect. Pebbled sand provides a natural earthy look, always attractive.

The surface of a finished sand candle is determined by the pouring temperature of the wax and the moisture content of the sand. The hotter the wax when you pour, the more it will seep into sand and result in a thick-walled candle.

To make a sand candle you'll need:
    Sand (10 or more pounds)
    Wax: medium melt point for candle, light melt point
      for the top
    Metal bucket or tub
    Water to moisten
    Wire rod stand-in for wick
    Spoon for digging
    Metal core wick
    Pliers
    Hot wax dip
    Cold water dip

Optional:
    Propane torch
    Color chips or powder

STANDARD STEP 1
Pouring temperature can be between 150° and 250°. (See color photos on next page for temperature effects.)

STEP 2
Place sand in metal bucket or tub. Dampen slightly with water and mix well until dry spots disappear. Sand should be just moist enough to hold a vertical wall so use water sparingly.

STEP 3
After the sand is moistened, spread it evenly around tub and pack it firmly with the palm of your hand.

STEP 4
Dig your hole with scoops, spoons—whatever works best for you. Dig clear through to the bottom of the container so the bottom of the candle will be flat. We're digging a perfectly round hole here but yours needn't be. Now is the time to decide the shape of your candle. Refine the inside surface wtih a small spoon and be sure no loose sand remains in the hole.

STEP 2

STEP 3

STEP 4

STEP 5

Determine the design of your candle at this stage. It should be well proportioned, not squatty, and you may add accessory objects now. We add a piece of driftwood and the part that is visible in the hole will be covered with wax. The part covered by—or resting in—sand will be visible in the final candle. This holds true for whatever materials or objects you add to sand candles.

STEP 6

Pour wax to roughly ¼ inch from top of sand. If you've used direct heat for melting, always transfer liquid wax to a pitcher for pouring. Return to container on stove to keep warm.

STEP 7

When wax in the hole begins to cloud, the top liquid will have receded a bit. Repour to original level. Driftwood is scarcely visible now in hole.

STEP 5

STEP 6

STEP 7

Pouring temperature can give your sand candle
a surface that resembles sturdy pottery or
delicate porcelain. The amount of sand retained
on the surface will pattern the glow (if any)
from the burning candle. The hotter the wax, the
denser the sand wall. Starting at the top, these
candles were poured at 150°, 170°, 190°,
220°, 250°.

STEP 8
When the top of the candle solidifies to a thickness of about ¼ inch, insert a wire where the wick will be. A piece of a metal coat hanger works well.

STEP 9
Remove candle from sand when wax is no longer warm to touch. Depending on size, it will take 3 hours or more for the candle to harden.

STEP 10
After the candle is thoroughly dry, brush loose sand from the surface and dip it in hot wax (270°) for two reasons: (a) for the practical purpose of preventing it from shedding sand; (b) for the aesthetic purpose of finishing the outside surface. This may also be accomplished by torching. (See Step 17.) Hold candle by wick wire or driftwood. An immediate plunge into cold water (after wax dip) will provide a gloss on the candle surface. (To show more designs, we're using a variety of candles to illustrate this and the following steps. But all procedures are in consecutive order.)

STEP 11
Remove wick wire. You might need pliers to separate it from hardened wax.

STEP 9

STEP 10

STEP 8

STEP 11

STEP 12
Cut wire-core wick about 3 inches longer than the candle depth. Dip about 2 inches of the cut wick into hot wax so that the cotton will not separate from the core as wick is pushed into the candle.

STEP 13
Once the wick is in, dig a hole about ¼ inch deep to expose possible hidden air pockets. Hole should be near, but not touching, the wick. A pen knife, ice pick or steak knife will do the job.

STEP 14
The top of your sand candle should be as perfect as you can make it. So, when you reach this stage, make sure the candle is level (you may want to use the skillet to level the candle as shown in Chapter 2) and pour a top at 200° to 210°. If you have used a 140-145° melt point wax, add hardening crystals for this final pour.

That's all there is to making a basic sand candle but who wants to stop there? Here are a few additional steps that will improve your finished candle.

STEP 13

STEP 14

STEP 12

STEP 15 (optional)
Remove the sand that sticks to driftwood, or other added materials, with a propane torch. This should be done before the candle is dipped into hot wax. (Step 11.)

STEP 16 (optional)
Using a propane torch to finish a sand candle is an alternative to dipping. With low flame, torch entire surface until wax is drawn through the sand. The right side of this candle has not yet been torched. Note the darker appearance of the left side where wax has already been drawn through.

STEP 17 (optional)
You can, of course, make your candle of colored wax. Even if you do, it can benefit from a swirled top. Here we're adding color powder ever so sparingly around the circumference of the candle. If you use solid color, shave it paper thin.

STEP 18
Supporting the candle in one hand, chase color around top with a propane torch. With low flame you can control both direction and intensity of color. Every effect you achieve will be interesting.

STEP 15

STEP 17

STEP 16

STEP 18

Great flexibility of design is a major advantage of sand casting. And with such inserts as driftwood and semi-precious stones, you can achieve interesting effects. Following are some of my sand candles.

This candle is notable first of all for its depth. Ability to accommodate different sizes and shapes is one of the greatest molding assets of sand. The driftwood placement is also unusual here in that it seems to grow out of the candle as wings and makes the finished work seem poised for flight.

An attractively shaded piece of agate becomes a window reflecting the glow of inside light in this small bowl-like sand candle. Note the distinct taper of the candle bottom. Agate rests on driftwood. Both were inserted before wax was poured into the sand cavity. This candle has been refilled six times. Outside surface has not been disturbed.

To make this three-tiered sand candle attached to a two-foot piece of driftwood, pour one level at a time and let cool. Bottom level will be covered with sand as you pour the next level. You can use a different sand each time. Tops are colored with chips and propane torch.

Precious and semi-precious stones find a compatible setting in sand and wax. The base of honey onyx is separate. The formation of the candle follows the wedge-cut lines of the base. A pair of agate slices and tower-like onyx in the back are imbedded candle wall.

When a driftwood-and-sand candle is too large to be dipped into hot wax for the finishing step, apply the wax (heated to 300°) with a paint brush. Wax adds a polished look to driftwood. Candle on the right was poured on a slate-colored stone base which was buried in the sand before the mold was formed. Heat stone with a torch before pouring so that it will adhere to the wax.

Your sand candle should be, first and foremost, well proportioned. There are no established rules for designing sand candles; the challenge is to your imagination. You also have freedom to determine texture through pouring temperature as well as choice of sand.

A common flaw is shedding of the sand surface. Let the candle remain in the sand for 24 hours. Then avoid additional shedding by dipping or torching the outside surface of the candle. Dipping adds gloss to the candle surface; torching gives it a matte finish. Take care also to pack the inside walls of your sand mold so that loose grains of sand will not invade the molten wax.

The top of your candle should show a smooth finish, whether or not you add decorative color. It takes patience to dig and shape a sand candle—don't finish it in haste. Some part of the top will be visible for as long as you use the candle.

Finally, the wick, or wicks, should be placed so that the candle will burn properly, and not consume the entire surface of the candle. A wall of wax should be retained. To refill the candle, you need only to pour a new center.

Hanging driftwood-and-sand candle shows off the kinetic quality of candlelight through a slice of agate imbedded on the side. When this candle is lifted out of the sand, the agate is completely covered with sand which you remove by torching. Locate wicks far enough away from agate so wax around edges of the stone will not melt.

IMPROVISED MOLDS
CHAPTER 4

You'll know you're a confirmed candlemaker when you view almost every object you see in terms of the candle it could hold or mold. For many people, improvised molds and container candles are the spice of candle-making and a never-ending preoccupation. They make serviceable candles and give you good reason to scout flea markets, thrift shops and garage sales. Even a visit to the supermarket holds rewards.

We're considering three broad categories of improvised molds: (1) Containers which become a permanent part of the candle—glasses, metal boxes, vases and the like; (2) disposable containers such as milk cartons, beverage bottles, food cartons; (3) reusable containers from which you'll release candles—drinking glasses, gelatin molds, and other unusually-shaped containers you probably have around the house.

Some of your container candles no doubt will be novelties you couldn't bear to light. But most will be the type you can use and enjoy indefinitely. It's best to use a low melt point wax so that the flame will clean the sides of the mold and the entire candle will be consumed by the burning wick. You can pour another candle into the same container. The temperature for pouring into permanent containers should be between 180° and 190°. Wax for other improvised molds which release the candle can be poured at temperatures up to 195°.

Our start-to-finish example is a container candle—the popular beer mug novelty. Then we'll go on to other techniques you'll find useful in creating candles personally yours.

For the beer mug candle you'll need:
    Low melt point wax
    Beer mug
    Metal wick tab
    Metal core wick
    Whipping bowl and beater
    Wax for whipping (½ pound)
    Color powder or chips
    Pliers
    Wire-cutting pliers
    Ice pick or dowel

For other examples shown you'll need:
    Tapered drinking glass
    Decorative bottle
    Large paper bag
    Hammer
    Milk carton
    Masking tape
    Wick wire
    Color as desired
    Corrugated cardboard (optional)

STANDARD STEP 1
Pour at 190°. Color wax to yellow shade of beer with yellow chips or powder. This candle takes about ¾ pound of yellow wax; ½ pound of clear wax for whipping.

STEP 2
Cut wire core wick about 3 inches higher than top of glass.

STEP 3
Thread wick through the bottom opening of the metal tab. With pliers, press prongs of the tab tightly against the wick to hold it securely. Do not squeeze the tab too hard or you will break the wire inside the wick.

STEP 4
Before pouring, rotate the glass in your hand for a few minutes or rinse it in hot water and dry thoroughly. Cold glass containers can crack from the shock of hot wax. Now, pour to about 2 inches from the top of the glass. Leave room for "suds."

STEP 5
Hold wick above the center of the poured wax and let it drop slowly to the bottom of the glass. Use an ice pick or dowel to make sure the tab is flat against the bottom of the glass. There's no need to repour a beer candle since it will be topped with whipped wax. When wax begins to harden, simply prick it with the ice pick or dowel to let air escape.

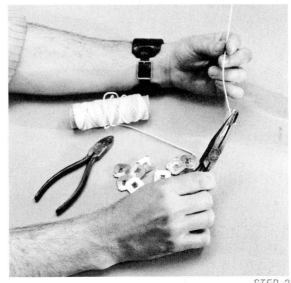

STEP 3

STEP 4

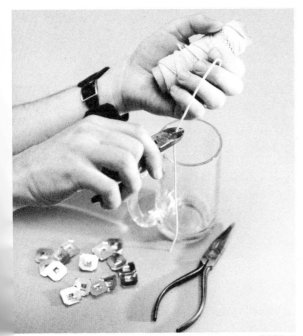

STEP 2

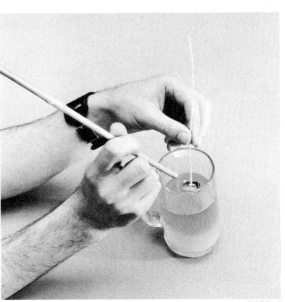

STEP 5

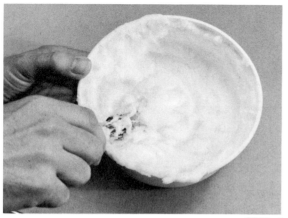

STEP 6

STEP 6

In a smaller pan (or 1 pound coffee can) heat clear wax and let it cool to melting point for whipping. For this, add ¼ teaspoon of hardening crystals to your ½ pound of wax.

Pour whipping wax into a container which is wider than it is deep. With wire whisk, fork or egg beater, fluff wax until it looks like lumpy whipped cream.

STEP 7

When the yellow wax has solidified and cooled, pile whipped wax to ½ inch or so above the top of the glass. Use a fork, or a spoon if you find it easier. Let some of the whipped wax drip over the top of the glass for a temptingly realistic effect.

STEP 7

Your finished candle is a delight to look at, if not to sample. The same procedure you've just used is adaptable for all familiar beverages—from hot chocolate to a root beer float. All you change is the glass and the color. You may want to insert a straw in some beverage candles. Do this when the wax is still soft and keep the straw well away from the wick.

GLASS MOLDS

Glass is so available and so appropriate for candles you'll find hundreds of ways to put it to use. All glass molds—reusable and disposable—provide a smooth and shiny surface finish that you won't get from any other mold; including metal. Use glasses that are slightly tapered and which have no lip at the top. Many consider a glass mold finish even superior to that of RTV Silicone Rubber. (See Chapter 6.)

Containers that become a part of the candle run the gamut from beer mugs and canning jars to salvaged bottles with their original labels or with chunks of glass glued to them.

STEP 1

STEP 2

STEP 3

Always remember to warm the glass before pouring; never pour at a temperature above 200°. Slight adaptations of the technique shown are required for different types of glass projects. Here are a few specific examples which apply generally to molds in these respective categories.

DRINKING GLASS

These are best among glass molds. Use a silicone release spray with glass, if you care to, but it's not vitally necessary. (See Metal Molds, Chapter 5.)

The top of the glass may be the top or the bottom of the candle; if the bottom of the glass is round, then it must be the top of the candle. Also, it's important to repour as soon as wax contracts noticeably, and to probe after each pouring to avoid air pockets around the wick.

STEP 1
This 6-ounce glass holds a little less than ½ pound of wax.

After measuring metal core wick against the side of the glass (allow an extra 3 inches when you cut) form a coil at the bottom by turning the wick in a spiral as shown. Bend the upright portion so that it is perpendicular to the coil and will stand straight.

STEP 2
Insert the wick with the coil at the center of the glass bottom. If the wick refuses to sit up straight, pour a few drops of wax to seal it. Bend the top of the wick around a wire or pencil to steady it and pour medium melt point wax. Repour as the wax contracts and probe once or twice to release air when wax begins to harden.

STEP 3
After wax has been poured use a dowel or ice pick to make sure the bottom of the wick is still centered and touching the bottom of the glass. Let the candle cool naturally, or use a room-temperature water bath.

Four to 6 hours later the candle can be removed from the glass. The coiled wick will be visible and easy to retrieve at the top of the candle.

If your candle doesn't just slide out quickly from a glass mold with gentle tapping, place the glass in the refrigerator for about ½ hour. Never put a candle in the freezer. Frigid temperature will cause cracks and ruin your candle.

THE FINISHED CANDLE . . .

was removed from the mold and received no further treatment. Burning wick emphasizes the surface sheen a glass mold produces. Also note the slight taper of the candle, remembering that the top of the candle was molded in the bottom of the glass.

Improvise molds you can discard. Pour a layered candle in a half-gallon milk carton (top shelf); achieve an embossed pattern by using a wine bottle. Pour a square column in a quart milk carton—decorate by torching color chips onto the plain surface. Pour a votive candle in a jelly glass. Pour into the halves of a rubber ball—and cover with whipped wax and glass chips—to make a candle to hold hors d'oeuvres.

Treasures in trash? The alertness that comes with candlemania helps you find them everywhere.

A wine bottle, fondly remembered for its original content; an empty perfume bottle that was too expensive to part with lightly; a pickle jar that has a certain jauntiness—all are candidates for more shining hours as candle containers or molds.

In most cases, the top opening of these molds will be too small to allow release of the candle. You'll smash the mold in order to display its wax likeness.

If at all possible, it's preferable to place the wick before pouring bottle molds, especially tall ones. Should this be too difficult, pour your candle and, when the wax has hardened and cooled completely, heat a metal rod (straightened coat hanger) and push it through the candle where the wick will be. When cool, remove the rod, dip the wire wick in liquid wax and insert it in the channel cleared by the rod.

STEP 1
Bottle is about 12 inches tall but wire core wick on a metal tab can be prodded until it stands straight.

STEP 2
If your aim is not steady enough to pour wax into a narrow bottle neck, improvise a paper funnel and let the wax slide down into the bottle. Or use a regular funnel. We're pouring up to the point where the bottle top begins to narrow, using 2 pounds of wax.

STEP 3
After the candle has set (in a water bath about 8 hours) place the bottle inside a large bag—or anything with three closed sides—and prepare to smash the bottle. Using a hammer, tap the bottom of the bottle gently until you hear cracking glass. If necessary, tap along sides. Be careful not to damage the surface of the candle by using hammer too forcefully.

STEP 1

STEP 2

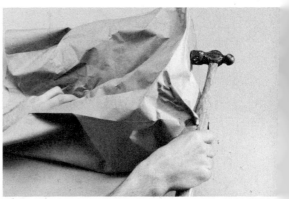

STEP 3

STEP 4

STEP 4

The candle emerges cleanly from the bag; glass can be put back into the bag and discarded. Trim the wick to ¾ inch. Note the giant raindrop shape of the candle. It isn't always necessary to pour to the top of an improvised glass mold. Your sense of proportion and composition will guide you to many surprising effects.

STEP 5

A candle of this shape invites a familiar kind of decoration—the dripping wax reminiscent of the bottle candles often found in Italian restaurants. Heat colored wax and let it cool to around 140°, or just to the melt point of your wax. Take a sharp knife and press notches around the top rim of the candle. Slits should be about ½ inch apart. Now, drip the colored wax lightly around the top edge of the candle and allow the wax to run down through the slits and onto the sides of the candle. Choose a dripping color to complement or contrast to the color of the candle itself.

STEP 5

THE FINISHED CANDLE . . .

your own recycling program in action! From now on you'll assay intended trash as carefully as a mint inspector examines coins.

IMPROVISED MOLDS

HOUSEHOLD CONTAINERS

The milk carton typifies a rich field for improvised molds, namely, many of the containers you use in cooking, and the commercial package containers of home equipment and foods. It's pointless to attempt to list these because you know best the resources of your kitchen and market basket.

Just to cite a few examples, molds for gelatin salads or cakes produce a versatile array of candles. Cup cake or other miniature molds, or muffin tins, are ideal for place marker candles for your children's birthday parties. You'll think of other ideas.

The surface finish of a candle made in a household container mold will usually leave something to be desired. Dipping comes to the rescue. Here are a few tips to remember.

To soften, or even remove, minor flaws, dip in hot wax (up to 270°). It's a good idea to have the wick wire or the wick itself in place to serve as a handle for the dip.

To add an almost opaque surface coating, or another color, dip in cooler wax (190-210°).

To add surface luster, dip in cold water immediately after any wax dip.

All dipping should be fast. The candle should be in wax or water no more than 2 or 3 seconds. Shake off excess wax after dipping. Never use the sink for a water bath or for dipping; the removal of congealed wax from a drain may cost more than all your candle equipment and supplies.

Is there any candlemaker who has never made a candle in a milk carton? On the suspicion that there isn't, we're going to show "something else" to do with this homey and usually available mold.

Incidentally, whenever you use a milk carton as a mold you can avert disaster by reinforcing the carton so that it will not bulge under the weight of poured wax.

A simple way is to place a strip of masking tape diagonally across the open top of the carton to straighten corners. (You'll remove the slanted top closure section of the carton before you do anything else.)

Another way is to construct a plywood box—or a corrugated housing for the carton. We're using scored paper board here. The fit should be just slack enough to allow easy placement and removal of the box over and from the carton.

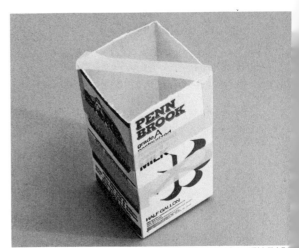

REINFORCING WITH TAPE

REINFORCING WITH BOX

STEP 1

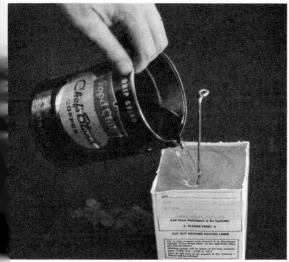

STEP 2

STEP 3

STANDARD STEP 1
Pour at 210°. Use separate pans for two or three colors, as desired. For this mold we are using 1¼ pounds of wax. Divide this total by the number of colors you want to use.

STEP 2
We've slanted the mold so that layers will be diagonal rather than straight. Rest the mold on or against anything that will tilt it without tipping it over. The picture shows the second color pouring which is made when the bottom pour is solid but still warm (about ½ hour between each pour).

STEP 3
Colored layers may be as wide or as narrow as you choose. But before you pour the top layer, straighten the mold and insert a wick wire in the center. Make your final pouring with the mold on a level surface.

THE FINISHED CANDLE . . .

Since you last saw the candle we've broken a rule by putting it into the refrigerator while the wax was still warm. We've also inserted the wick and removed the candle by tearing away the carton. What you see in this finished candle are indeed thermal cracks but in sufficient quantity to provide an interesting effect. The slanted layers form a geometric pattern and the cracks simulate alligatored pottery or marbling—a good way to compensate for any mold which doesn't provide a perfect surface finish.

When wick wires are placed in wax that is still soft they will be embedded as the wax sets. When you first cut the metal rods, make it a habit to bend the top in some fashion. This will serve as a helping handle when it's time to remove the wire from the hardened wax.

Another generally useful tool for container candles is a bottle cutter. We found one by Fleming in the dime store. A bottle cutter is a good investment because it will widen the scope and uses of glass containers.

With the Fleming cutter we've removed the top from an imported wine bottle, leaving the label intact, and poured a candle that's appropriate for a den or recreation room. Coating the label with a clear varnish or acrylic will preserve it, no matter how often you refill the inside.

This sconce candle by David Morseth, shows ingenious use of a wine bottle top. The cork is in place at the bottom of the candle. A piece of driftwood, from which a natural knot has been removed, serves as the candle holder. The driftwood is attached to the wall plaque with two screws.

STANDARDS OF EXCELLENCE

Unless you specifically want it to, your finished candle need not look as if it came from an improvised mold. This is a test of your technical skill as well as your ability to select appropriate molds.

If you've used a glass mold your candle should have a virtually perfect surface. The mold itself assures this if you've followed the rules—poured hot, clean wax into a clean mold, repoured carefully, and extracted the candle with a minimum of fingerprints.

The surface of candles from cardboard or other paper molds will almost always need some finishing treatment. (See Chapter 9 for decorating techniques.) Polishing with a nylon stocking should always be the final touch.

Color can be a problem in improvised molds; be frugal with it. Deep or intense colors are better used in metal or rubber molds.

Many of your improvised molds will produce novelty candles. But if you are serious about the craft, you must recognize the difference between novelty candles and those which can improve your technical ability. Pour plain shapes and concentrate on color and surface quality.

Hanging wok candle should be suspended high enough to let you enjoy the color-streaked design and the translucent glow when lighted.

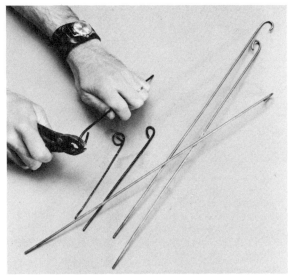

BENDING WICK WIRE

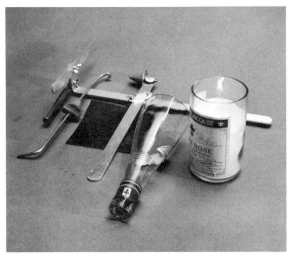

BOTTLE CUTTER

SCONCE CANDLE

METAL MOLDS
CHAPTER 5

Metal-mold candles are to candlemaking what the classics are to music and literature—basic forms and techniques, crystallized by the virtuosity of the composer.

To be a complete candlemaker, you should refine your skills to the highest degree by using metal molds often. Candles molded in metal will reflect not only the precision of the mold, but also the quality of the wax and your meticulous handling of it. Taking pains is literally the secret of molding perfect candles in metal. More than anything else, this means cleanliness—from the condition of the mold to the straining of the wax, to your handling of the finished candle.

Metal molds merit scrupulous workmanship because they're capable of producing the purest expression of your craftsmanship. You'll probably want to own an assortment of metal molds in different sizes and shapes. But, if you want to invest in only one at the outset, choose a hurricane metal mold because it will serve for many types of candles—ice, hurricanes, layered, color block and solids. A hurricane mold has no hole in the bottom so you'll handle wicking as you do in container candles.

The normal translucence of petroleum wax will be apparent in a metal-mold candle, so add hardening crystals in the suggested ratio if you want a pure white candle. If you plan to use color, omit the crystals. Do not use crystals for the outer layer of a twice-poured candle because they will make the wax too dense to reveal the inside color.

A new material enters your candle vocabulary now—silicone release, needed for metal molds. This is a liquid silicone lubricant, packaged in aerosol form and available in most hobby shops. Absolutely essential for metal molds, silicone release can also be used on improvised molds.

Since all metal molds pouring is basic, we'll show one complete procedure and then demonstrate how slight alterations can produce strikingly different candles.

For a metal-mold candle you'll need:

> Medium melt point wax
> Basic round mold
> Release spray
> Cotton wick
> Masking tape
> Floral clay
> Metal wick pin (nail)
> Wick holder—rod or pencil
> Ice pick or puncture stick
> Knife
> Skillet
> Nylon stocking
> Color or hardening crystals
> Water bath

For the twice-poured star and block candle:
> Star mold
> Color
> Color blocks
> Cookie sheet (optional)

METAL MOLDED CANDLES

William E. Webster, Ph.D., Professor of Philosophy, Philadelphia College of Art, discusses metal mold candles in his shop in downtown Philadelphia. Currently his personal enthusiasm is for sand and hurricane candles, but he believes that metal molds are invaluable in helping the beginning candlemaker perfect his craftsmanship.

A giant candle weighing 30 pounds becomes the center of interest in a plant window. It is poured in a handmade metal mold and uses up chunks of imperfect and damaged candles. (Cathy's Candle Cupboard)

STANDARD STEP 1

Pour at 190-195°. This candle takes 2 pounds of wax.

STEP 2

Clean your mold before or after every pouring. Run very hot water over the outside of the mold until all leftover wax on the inside has melted. Then wipe the inside of the mold with a terry towel to remove any wax. Use a ruler or long stick to reach bottom. With this way of cleaning no wax will go down the drain.

STEP 3

Spray release into mold. A quick spritz will release enough silicone mist to coat the inside surface. Too much spray will leave an oily film on the candles. Excess release may be wiped off with a clean, soft cloth. Turn the mold upside down and thread the wick through the hole in the bottom.

STEP 4

Tying the wick knot, which will remain outside the bottom of the mold after the wick is threaded through the hole, is an art in itself. Hold the end of the wick and make a loop; with wick continuing under the section you're holding, make another loop. You'll have a horizontal figure 8. From the left, slip your wick pin (a nail) into the center of the left loop, covering inner sides of both loops. Pull the hanging part of the wick to tighten the loops around the pin.

STEP 2

STEP 3

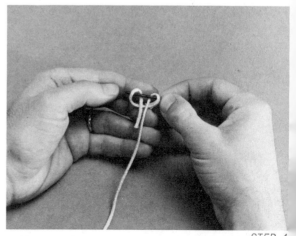

STEP 4

40

STEP 5
Take a small piece of floral clay and wrap it around the wick at the center of the pin. Then cut two strips of masking tape and place them so that they will overlap at the wick hole. Pull the wick from the long end (at the top of the mold) until the knot, floral clay and pin are tight against the hole. Photo shows how the bottom of the mold should look when this operation is completed. The order of materials, from the mold outward: masking tape, floral clay and knotted pin.

STEP 6
Turn the mold right side up and wrap the top of the wick around a pencil or slim rod. Use a simple knot to hold the wick taut.

STEP 7
Stir the wax, strain it if you wish, and pour at 190° to 195° to about ½ inch from the top of the mold. Let the mold sit for 2 or 3 minutes to allow time for the wax to warm the metal. Tap the mold lightly around the sides with a pencil to release air.

STEP 8
Using a potholder, grasp the top of the hot mold and place it in a room-temperature water bath. (Water level should be the same as that of the liquid wax in the mold.)

STEP 5

STEP 7

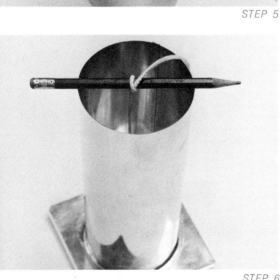

STEP 6

STEP 8

STEP 9

As soon as a drop in the wax level is noticed, repour immediately. (This will happen in less than 5 minutes after pouring.) Timing of the first repour is important; if it is delayed, the edge of the finished candle will crumble. Additional repours may be made every 20 or 30 minutes until the wax stops contracting. Never repour above the level of the previous pour. Repouring temperature can be between 180° and 210°. Let the mold sit in the water bath until it cools—this could be 2 or more hours, depending on the size of the candle.

STEP 10

During the cooling process—but before the wax has hardened—keep the top open with an ice pick or metal rod. Penetrate the wax to the liquid inside. The purpose of this is to get rid of air pockets which may have formed within the candle. Repour this cavity.

STEP 11

When the mold is no longer warm to the touch, remove it from the water bath and pull out the wick pin at bottom. It will slip through the loops of the knot. Let the candle remain in the mold for another hour or two until it has completely cooled to the touch. Remove pencil from the top of the wick.

STEP 12

To remove the candle from the mold, rotate the mold in your hands, kneading it gently. Then, turn the mold upside down—the candle should slide into your hand. If the candle doesn't come out easily, put the mold into the refrigerator for no longer than ½ hour.

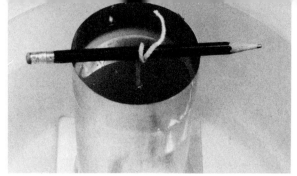

STEP 9

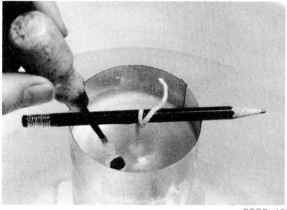

STEP 10

STEP 11

STEP 12

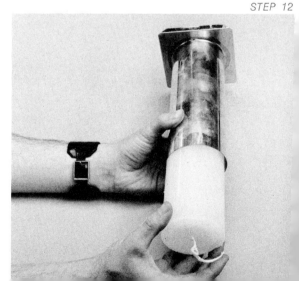

STEP 13
Once the candle is out of the mold, trim the wick at top, leaving about ½ inch exposed. Remember, the bottom of the mold is the top of the candle.

STEP 14
With a paring knife, dig into the bottom of the candle about ½ inch and cut the bottom of the wick.

STEP 15
The seam of the mold will be visible on the side of the candle. Scrape lightly with a paring knife until the telltale line disappears. For a smooth finish, let the weight of the knife ride on your thumb, not on the candle.

STEP 16
Place the candle bottom down on a skillet over low heat (about 225°). Rotate the candle in the palms of your hands until the bottom is leveled.

STEP 17
Fingerprints dull the surface of a candle. After all finishing touches have been completed, polish the candle lightly with a nylon stocking. Set the candle aside to age for a day or so before you light it.

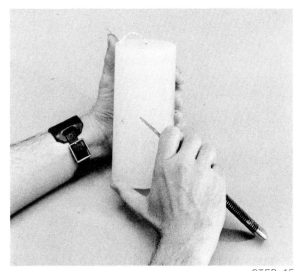
STEP 15

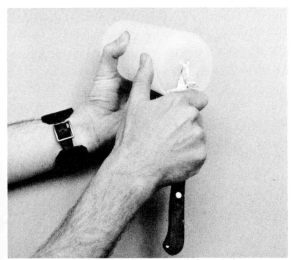
STEP 13

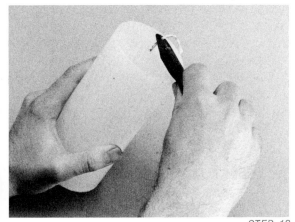
STEP 16

STEP 14

STEP 17

STEP 1

STEP 2

STEP 3

The preceding steps comprise the basic technique for all solid candles poured in metal molds. But any number of variations are possible, so a metal mold in itself should not restrict your imagination. The layered candle made in a milk carton in Chapter 4 is one departure. Block, or chunk, candles and twice-poured candles are two more appealing possibilities. Once you know the techniques for these you'll be able to structure original concepts.

STEP 1 — BLOCK CANDLE
Prepare the mold with release spray and secure the wick at top and bottom. Fill the mold with 1-inch wax squares (or irregular chunks) in one or more colors. Add color blocks to within 1 inch of the top. While doing this, be sure to keep the wick centered. If you want spaces between colors, simply place white blocks among the others. (Leftover wax, or the wax from leveling candles, may be used.)

STEP 2
Pouring at 230° will give a slightly opaque surface and much bleeding of color. If you want a more defined surface, and less color bleeding, pour at a lower temperature—but not lower than 200°. Pour clear wax (no crystals added) to the same level or a bit above the color blocks. Tap the mold lightly to release air.

STEP 3
Placing the filled mold into the water bath will stop the spreading of color. If you want strongly blended color, wait about 3 or 4 minutes. If you want sharper definition of color, use the water bath immediately after pouring.

STEP 4 (optional)
The finished appearance of the candle will determine your next move. If there's too much wax on the outside, a quick dip in hot wax (250-270°) will lessen opacity. If color seems too close to the surface, a dip in cool wax (190-210°) will provide some density to cover.

STEP 4

STEP 1

DO IT YOURSELF COLOR

If you are unable to find packaged color blocks for block or chunk candles, you can use wax scraps you've saved, or you can mold your own blocks in your own colors.

STEP 1
Spray a cookie sheet with silicone release and pour colored wax heated just until it becomes liquid. Depth of the pour is not important—½ inch or more will do. Let the wax cool.

STEP 2
When the wax is about the consistency of fudge, cut the wax horizontally and vertically with a dull knife.

STEP 3
After the wax hardens, turn the cookie sheet upside down and blocks will come apart easily. We're showing 3-inch blocks which will be broken into jagged pieces for a future chunk candle. If you like, you can score your wax into units of any size or shape. Store each color in individual containers.

STEP 2

STEP 3

TWICE-POURED STAR

STEP 1
Heat 2½ pounds of medium melt point wax to 195°.
Spray the mold with silicone release, secure the wick,
and pour to ½ inch from the top of the mold.

STEP 2
Run a long wire down each point of the star to release
trapped air and place in a water bath until wax at the
sides of the mold is about ⅛ to ¼ inch thick (or when
the wax starts to scum on top). Wipe water from mold,
then pour out liquid wax from the center of the mold.
(Return this wax to the heating pan; it can be reused.)
Photo shows the thickness of the wall of wax retained
in the mold.

STEP 3
Immediately pour a dark-colored wax (1½ pounds) into
the cavity of the mold at 180°. Allow the mold to sit just
long enough for colored wax to adhere to the white wax.
Place the mold back in a water bath to cool.

THE FINISHED CANDLE . . .

shows the effect of a light-dark color combination as
edges appear to be frosted. We've used a white wax
outside with a deep royal blue inside. Complementary or
contrasting combinations may be used but always use
the lighter color for the first, or outside pour.

Metal-mold candles are intrinsically complete as they
come from the mold, distinguished only by color and
shape. (They must be leveled.) Interior or exterior em-
bellishments are always optional but can be quite attractive. See decorative ideas for metal molds in Chapter 9.

Metal molds test your skill because they reveal your precision—or lack of it—in every process from mixing wax,
to adding color, to pouring properly.

Some of the most common surface flaws and their causes
are: cracks from a too-cold water bath, pit marks from
dust or wax particles in the mold, bubbles from air not
released.

In layered candles, each layer must partially harden before the next layer is poured or you will have excessive
color bleeding. But if a layer hardens completely before
the next pour you will have separation cracks which
weaken the candle. The temperature of each pour must
be the same or you will have uneven texture.

STEP 1

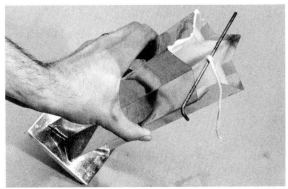

STEP 2

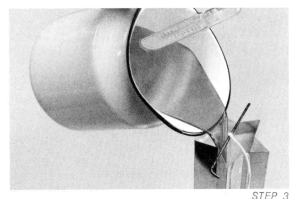

STEP 3

FINISHED CANDLE

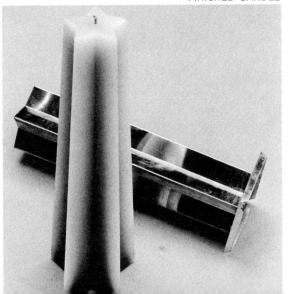

*Star-shaped metal mold candles in blue have
variety because of the way they were poured.
The six-pointed star uses a single pour of blue;
the five-pointed stars are twice-poured—one in
white with blue core, the other in green and blue.
(Cathy's Candle Cupboard)*

MAKE YOUR OWN RUBBER MOLDS
CHAPTER 6

A fairly recent innovation in candlemaking is the use of an industrial compound known as RTV Molding Rubber to make molds of astounding accuracy and sensitivity. With RTV it is possible to reproduce almost any object of reasonable size, in minute detail even to your own thumbprint on the model!

RTV has launched many new trends in candles, among them antique glass replicas, miniature animals and scores of novelties which, until now, were impossible to mold.

With the availability of materials such as Dow Chemical's RTV Silastic series or other molding rubbers from other manufacturers such as General Electric, hand-made rubber molds are within the capability of the amateur candlemaker. A word of warning: RTV is expensive, so be sure you really want to go into rubber molds. Beyond this advice, we give you nothing but encouragement. I have molded a three-foot African tusk, a totem pole, and a Venus de Milo, among other objects.

RTV is used in two parts—the compound itself, and a catalyst blended for curing. The ratio is 10 parts RTV to 1 part catalyst for normal curing. Also required are patience, attention to every detail and a willingness to experiment. The results are worth the effort you invest. An RTV mold will last through hundreds of pourings without loss of finished quality.

A flat, smooth work surface is advisable for making RTV rubber molds. For reasons which will be apparent, glass is a good choice. The illustrated section which follows details the molding of a small antique cut-glass toothpick holder. Except for the size of the mother mold, the procedure I'm going to show is the same for molding any object of your choice.

You'll need:
    RTV Silastic A (including catalyst)
    Medium melt point wax
    Bowl for mixing
    Two teaspoons
    Floral or modeling clay
    Toothpicks
    Rubber band
    Razor blade or knife
    Small towel

STEP 1
Apply floral clay to the entire top rim of the model. Peel off excess so that clay does not interrupt the design of the glass or protrude beyond the edge.

STEP 2
Turn the model upside down and press it firmly to the work surface.

STEP 3
The mother mold can be any container large enough to fit over the model with ½-inch margin at top and sides. We're using a food storage container and have sawed off bottom so that both ends are open.

STEP 4
Press floral clay around top edges of the mother mold.

STEP 1

STEP 3

STEP 2

STEP 4

STEP 5

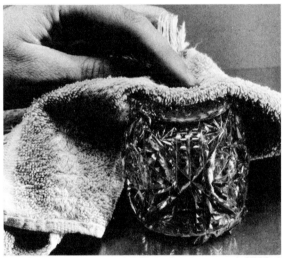

STEP 6

STEP 7

STEP 5
Before adhering mother mold to the work surface, measure it against the model and draw a line on the inside surface and outside to indicate the level of the ½ inch margin above the model.

STEP 6
Clean and dry the model thoroughly to remove all finger-prints from handling.

STEP 7
Center the mother mold over the model and press it firmly to the work surface.

STEP 8
Count out 10 tablespoons of RTV Silastic A into the mixing bowl. (We're using an inexpensive plastic dog food bowl that can be reused.)

STEP 9
Measure 1 tablespoon of catalyst from the tube into the bowl and mix thoroughly. Always use slow catalyst for deep curing (as shown in the picture). The more catalyst you use the faster the mold will cure.

STEP 10
Pour the rubber and catalyst mixture into the mother mold, letting it run down over the model.

STEP 11
Continue pouring until compound reaches level of the ½-inch margin line you made. Let mold stand 24 hours for curing. Let excess rubber cure in mixing bowl. Then peel it off.

STEP 8

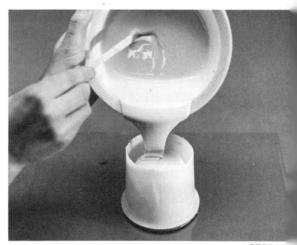

STEP 1

STEP 9

STEP

STEP 12
The next day, cut the excess material from the top of the
mother mold with a sharp knife so that it is level with the
top of the poured RTV.

STEP 13
With a small saw, slit the side of the mother mold to
remove it from the cured rubber.

STEP 14
With a sharp knife, slit rubber mold down the side and
halfway around the bottom of the model. Try to cut along
a line in the pattern of the model.

STEP 15
Open the slit rubber mold and the model will be easy to
remove.

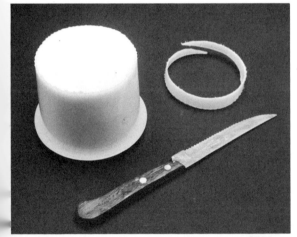

STEP 12

STEP 14

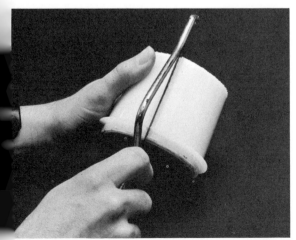

STEP 13

STEP 15

STEP 16

STEP 16
Drill a small hole through the center bottom of the rubber mold for the wick. We're using a $\frac{1}{16}$-inch bit.

STEP 17
Insert the wick using a jeweler's screwdriver or thin guide wire with a flattened end to push the wick through the hole. No release spray is necessary. Put the rubber mold back into the mother mold.

STEP 18
Place a heavy rubber band around the mother mold, near the bottom, to keep the slit in the mold from opening. Pour at 210°. (RTV molds can stand heat up to 600°.) Repour as you would a metal-mold candle.

STEP 19
Remove the candle from the mold—it practically pops out. The pattern of the glass is reproduced in every detail and you can repeat this feat as often as you wish.

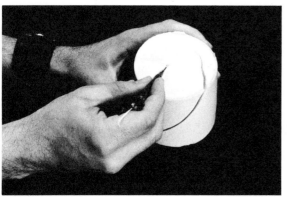

STEP 17

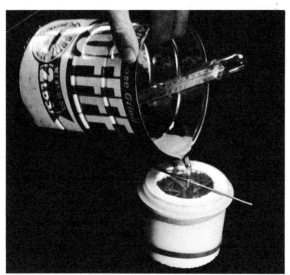

STEP 18

STEP 19

Novelty candles are more often designed for one-time use at special occasions than for permanent enjoyment. Rubber molds make it easy to duplicate animals or plants. Corn candles have shucks cut from sheets of honeycomb wax. Ears of sorghum are highlighted with gold Rub 'n Buff. (Cathy's Candle Cupboard)

STANDARDS OF EXCELLENCE

Rubber molds reproduce as exactly as a mirror reflects. When you make a rubber mold be sure the model is perfectly clean—devoid even of fingerprints.

Many of the flaws in a rubber mold candle can be traced to the mold itself. Surface air bubbles mean trapped air when the mold was made. Thin spots in the design indicate poor quality of molding rubber or a bad seam.

A rubber mold candle must glow when burning or the effort of reproducing the design will have been to no avail. Don't use wax additives or the density of the candle will restrict its glow. The melt point of the wax should be no higher than 142°.

Dark or too-intense color will also reduce candle glow, so add color carefully to the wax and test it before pouring. (See Chapter 1.)

THE NEXT STEP

Our model was almost a miniature in cut glass but size is no problem for rubber mold reproduction—the tall vase could as easily be duplicated. The small piece of woodcarving is shown as a reminder that glass is only one of the materials you can mold successfully in RTV rubber.

If air bubbles appear near the surface of the poured candle, warm the mold in the oven (low, 175°) before you pour future candles.

RTV manufacturers issue specification sheets for proper handling of the material. Write for one to increase your confidence in using it. When working with RTV rubber, always follow specifications on the package.

EASY-TO-MAKE PLASTER MOLDS
CHAPTER 7

A plaster mold will not capture the fine detail so precisely reproduced by a rubber mold, but to the serious candle-maker, handmade plaster molds offer excitement as well as challenge.

Plaster molds are easy and inexpensive to make—and they'll broaden the scope of your creativity because there are numerable objects which can be molded in plaster. And once you produce a candle in plaster you can duplicate it a hundred times or more, if you wish, because these molds are durable and reliable.

Objects with a smooth surface are best for molding in plaster but contours present no problem. Our demonstration model is a Carlsberg bottle with a faint but distinctive curving profile. The model for the hurricane globe in Chapter 8 was a glass globe.

You make a plaster mold in two parts and the most crucial step is to place the model *exactly* halfway into the first plaster poured. Model in the demonstration is placed horizontally. But the finished mold will be turned upright for pouring. Measure your model to find the halfway mark and draw a line around it with a felt-tip pen.

Plaster costs in the neighborhood of 10 cents a pound, so you can afford to experiment. I find U.S. Gypsum Ultracal 30 to be the best molding plaster available. Look for it in 50-pound bags—a more economical buy than smaller packages. Ask for Ultracal 30 at lumberyards or check the phone book for a U.S. Gypsum distributor.

You'll build a four-sided wood frame to hold the poured plaster. Set it on a smooth work surface—glass is probably best. It's a good idea to avoid cutting the wood pieces to the exact size of the model, even though you'll nail them together in the dimensions needed. Cutting longer pieces will enable you to use the wood again and again for models of different sizes.

Almost anyone can make a plaster mold; don't let the following equipment intimidate you.

To make the small plaster mold pictured you'll need:

> Plaster—fill a 1-pound can
> Plastic bucket
> Mixing spoon
> Water—1-pound coffee can half full
> Hammer
> Saw
> Miter box (optional)
> Wood—4 strips, ¾-inch pine
> Soft brush
> Lard or shortening
> Wicking
> Two marbles
> Glass or other smooth work surface

STEP 1
Assemble your materials. You'll notice that we're using a 1-pound can of loosely packed plaster and that we have already sawed and nailed the wood form to the proper size for the model.

STEP 2
Using lard or solid shortening, lubricate all parts of the wood form which the plaster will touch. Lubricate the model, too. This close-up shows how oversized boards are joined to provide the form for the model. The depth of the wood should be at least 1 inch more than half the depth of the model.

STEP 3
Model set horizontally in the form illustrates proper placement. One end rests against one side of the frame and will be the top of the finished mold. Allow a 1½ - inch margin around the other three sides of the model.

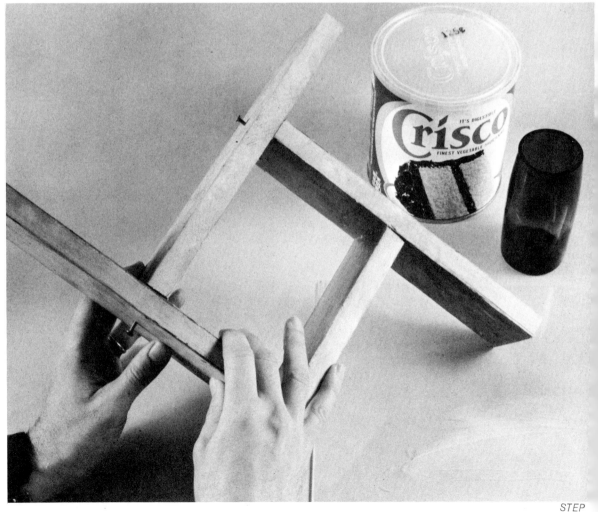